Praise Therapy

How I Use Biblical Mindfulness to Alleviate Anxiety, Depression, and Fear from My Life

By Jeraleen M. Ray

PRAISE THERAPY

ISBN 978-0-578-44677-6

Be advised, all Scriptures are from the King James Version unless otherwise noted.

From the rising of the sun unto the going down of the same the LORD'S name is to be praised.
Psalms 113:3

Table of Contents

Dedication

This book is dedicated foremost to my Lord and Savior Jesus Christ, and is written for the praise of His glory.

> Psalm 119:11: *Let the words of my mouth and the meditation of my heart be acceptable in Your sight, oh Lord, my strength and my redeemer!*

To my children, Darmon, Alfred, Lemuel, and Danielle, whose lives forced me to question and evaluate my own.

> Psalm 127:3: *Children are a gift from the LORD; they are a reward from him.*

Acknowledgements

Cover and Interior Design by Charmane Anegbe

Editing by Charmane Anegbe

Photography by Aaron Guyton

Published by Crimson Word Publishing

Foreword

There are numerous books on the market dealing with various types of therapies. As a Doctor of Christian Counseling, I have read and used many of them over the years. However, this book fits the spiritual counseling model wherein I have achieved the greatest successes. The book "Praise Therapy" brings an element of real-world spiritual effectiveness into the conversation on mental and emotional healing.

As a Licensed Clinical Social Worker and CEO of Wisdom Tree Counseling, Jeraleen draws on her many years as a health care professional and her personal spiritual experiences, to give the reader wealth of insight into the dynamics of what it takes to make "Praise, Faith and Gratefulness" a legitimate part of the therapeutic process. One of the most intimate and touching elements of the book is that it speaks to her own vulnerability in a series of transparent disclosures which reveal how she has had to survive and overcome challenging, personal situations in her own past.

"Praise Therapy" is unapologetic in its core belief that having a healthy, personal relationship with God in times of crisis is the best form of mental assurance. It is impossible to read this book and not be energized by its message.

Dr. Curtis Dodson, Word Wise Ministries

Preface

This book is written from my personal life experience of overcoming the challenges that I faced with unforgiveness, and the spirit of heaviness (also known as depression, worry, shame, guilt, and fear). It is centered on my Christian faith perspective formed over the past 40 years that includes the discipline of prayer, reading, and studying the Bible, then meditating and applying biblical truth and trust in God to my life. It is not meant to be a catch-all or cure-all approach for everyone. It is my testimony of how praise healed my life.

This book is intended specifically to help those who suffer from situational and environmental trauma, and for those who don't have the privilege of healthcare or the financial means to pay for mental health counseling and treatment services. If you or someone you know is struggling with anxiety, fear, anger, or depression, and needs a proven way to push back against the hopelessness and despair they are experiencing, then read this book.

Praise Therapy is the way God blessed my life to manage, overcome, and defeat the down pull of negative thoughts and emotions that had entrapped my soul and undermined my life's potential and purpose. I didn't even know it was therapy. I just wanted to get better clarity and understanding about my life and not be sucked into the under tow of drug addiction, alcoholism, and mental illness that had affected my family for generations.

"Father I stretch my hands to thee; no other help I know."

It all started with me crying out to God and asking many investigative questions about who I was. Why am I this way? Why is my life so messed up? How do I handle being lonely and isolated? Why do I make decisions that hurt me? What happened to me? Despite the things that happened to me emotionally and physically why do I still have faith? Why don't I give up? How do I keep going when my life is upside down? What gives me the internal stamina and strength to go on? What pushes me and drives my life to keep me resilient? How did I continue to have hope when I had no money, friends, or support of family?

Praise Therapy includes my personal, professional, and spiritual experiences. It will express how I've finally chosen to live my life. I've thought about writing this book for a long time, but I really didn't know how to present the book. Should it be for Christian believers only? Since I'm proposing a therapy to address overcoming mood and thought disorders, should I write it from a humanist, or a secular perspective? Was I only to address the overwhelming assault that many people face who suffer with pain, anxiety, fear, and depression? Or did I want to share the practical benefits of daily praising God from my experience?

After much consideration, I discovered that all the above questions were interrelated, and all of the approaches were a part of my healing process and life experience. Therefore, I will honor the entire process; all of it. Every step that I took, sometimes forward and many times backwards, was all a part of Praise Therapy. My conclusion is that ***Praise Therapy* is an integrated spiritual mindfulness approach**, or the means by which I came to really understand, in the words of my wise ancestors, that "God is a heart fixer and mind regulator."

Praise Therapy is the spiritual catalyst that changed my mentality and the concept of how I thought of and viewed myself in my heart.

Proverbs 27:3: *As a man thinketh in his heart so is he.*

Introduction

Forces beyond your control can take away everything you possess except one thing, your freedom to choose how you will respond to the situation.

Viktor Frankel

Welcome to Praise Therapy

Victor Frankel survived the torture and injustice of Nazi prison camps during WWII. He examined his experience, then later wrote about how he survived the horrors of that experience in his book, *Man's Search for Meaning*. Like Mr. Frankel, I found myself having to search for meaning and understanding of how to live my life in a healthy productive way, even though the circumstances and situations of my life were awful and sometimes of my own doing. *Praise Therapy* is the spiritual choice I made to gain the tenacity to effectively manage my life.

This book evolves from my personal life experiences of early childhood sexual and emotional abuse, poverty, and neglect, and as an adult having numerous failed relationships, persevering through homelessness, divorce, parenting four children alone, all while living with the historical and ongoing trauma of racism and economic injustice.

This book tells in part how I confronted the evil mental weight of oppression that came against me in my thoughts and feelings, to pervert and take away my life force to the point where I didn't know who I was, what I wanted, or how to live as the person God intended me to be.

Spirituality and the field of mental health have one common major goal, and that is to alleviate emotional suffering; to liberate and blossom the self. A major goal of mankind for ages has been to seek liberation from suffering, both physical and mental. Every civilization, culture, and society have their unique solutions to deal with suffering. Almost all ancient civilizations had a strong belief in God, soul, and spirituality, and maintained well established means and methods through which spiritual enlightenment could be attained. Western culture placed labels on these processes called religion and philosophy.

For example, in western medicine treatment is focused only on the physical body, and areas of functioning are addressed separately. Most researchers and scientists look at one part of the person and address one organ at a time. This means you will see a cardiologist for your heart, urologist for your bladder, and a nephrologist for your kidneys. Treatment is directed to the parts of the body they can observe, measure, and quantify.

Praise Therapy addresses the part of human existence that can't be quantified, easily observed or measured... like the effects of cultural impact, hope, determination, faith, and resilience. Then these areas are dismissed as being unscientific, mystical, or spiritual, and placed in the category of religion and philosophy.

In the purest wisdom there were no labels, only a clear sense of human need for the whole person to be loved, nurtured, valued, and cared for.

Examples like a crushed spirit devoid of hope, or severe aggression due to hatred, murderous anger, self-mutilation, unrelenting worry, and isolating fear are described as mental illness. Then due to the shame and stigma of mental illness, the suffering is denied, never talked about, and not addressed. The impression is given that mental illness is beyond understanding and the most effective treatment is to drug or lock the person away to control it.

A Different Perspective

The holistic view I present in this book takes a different perspective, a God perspective of the WHOLE PERSON, and views the whole self of a person as a viable spirit that dwells in a physical body that lives in relationship with and to other people in the earth's environment. This holistic perspective takes into consideration the spirit of a person, the whole context of their spirituality, culture, and environment. This perspective further recognizes that your spirituality is an important part of who you are as a person, and no lasting healing can take place without addressing your body, soul and spirit.

As a 7th generation descendant of Africans who were enslaved and in the United States of America, I have had to learn to embrace and love myself while living with layers of stigma, shame, sadness and sorrow in silence. This is a physically lonely isolating experience even though there are numerous others who are affected the same way. I believe this is where my depression comes from. However, when I see myself as a child of God with unlimited access to love grace, mercy and forgiveness this is a spiritual perspective that removes the stigma, doubt and fear and creates the hopeful expectation that my thoughts, feelings, and emotions can be effectively addressed.

My cultural, relational, and spiritual orientation comes from a very diverse African American, Judeo-Christian perspective, centered on strong faith, family, education, and working-class values created while I was growing up and living in the metropolitan inner-city area of Los Angeles, California. All of these influences shaped me into the person I am today. After everything I've experienced, what I want to share in this book is how my faith and trust in the Bible and the God of the Bible has kept me whole and healthy, not without pain and suffering, but with a clear sense that I am loved, forgiven, nurtured, and cared for by God.

> 2 Timothy 1:7: *God has not given us a spirit of fear, but of power and of love and of a sound mind.*

According to the above scripture, God gives us the spiritual power that removes fear and gives the ability to love right and act with the best mentality and principles of reason. According to the scripture through his love, God has graced my life not with fear, but with mental strength and wellness. For the praise of His glory. He urged me to write this book just for you, so that you might grow in faith. God wants you to go from being overwhelmed to overflowing with His presence, power, and purpose in your life.

Right now, you might be asking questions too. How can I praise God the way my life is? How can I sing a song of praise today? I want to encourage you to stop asking questions and follow the Nike directive—Just Do It. Lift up your head, hands, and heart to God. Let the transformative power of the Holy Spirit elevate your soul and spirit. Transcend every earthly down pull and be lifted up to heavenly places where Christ is seated.

> Psalm 24:7: *Lift up your heads, O ye gates; and be ye lifted up, ye everlasting doors; and the King of glory shall come in.*

Author's Disclaimer

I gained the healing effect of *Praise Therapy* through the spiritual discipline that comes from hearing, reading, studying, and meditating on biblical scripture – The Holy Bible – then developing a hopeful perspective, using faith and obedience to apply scripture to my life.

Many books and research studies indicate mindfulness and meditation practices are helpful in treating anxiety, depression, and fear; for example, *A Course in Miracles, The Battlefield of Your Mind, The Power of Positive Thinking*. However, this book is written from my personal perspective of how specifically meditating on biblical scripture and applying it to my life changed my mentality and behavior.

My declaration is that *Praise Therapy* works for me every day and I'm humble enough to admit that praise therapy may not work for everyone; but I sincerely hope it will help and benefit every reader of this book.

Praise Therapy does not exclude the benefit and support gained through professional counseling and therapy. If you are being treated by a healthcare professional, or currently taking medication for a mental health diagnosis, consult your treating professional. The information in *Praise Therapy* should not be used to replace the specialized training and professional judgement of healthcare or mental healthcare professionals.

If you suspect that you are facing mental-health related problems, you are strongly encouraged to seek professional help.

Please seek help immediately

- if you have thoughts of killing (or otherwise harming) yourself or others,
- if you are gravely disabled (unable to care for yourself),
- if you are abusing substances, or
- if you or someone else is in any danger of harm.

Call National Alliance for the Mentally Ill-NAMI Helpline 1-800-950-NAMI.

Chapter 1

Acting on Emotional Pain

I wanted to kill my husband, and through tears I had picked up the lamp to slam it into his skull while he laid in bed asleep. In a quick second I aimed instead at the area above his head and saw my beautiful blue ginger jar lamp explode into pieces over him. This of course startled him from a sound sleep. Overwhelmed by my rage, I immediately ran out of the house and started to walk the streets of South-Central Los Angeles at two o'clock in the morning. I didn't know where I was going; I was angry, frightened by my own murderous thoughts, and just lost, not knowing what to do. I didn't think about my safety; I just kept walking.

I was hurt, perplexed, and overwhelmed, but the walking helped calm me down. The rage that had been in me earlier had been caused by the frustration and emotional pain I felt. It started that morning when I had gone to the credit union to withdraw the money to make our mortgage payment. I filled out the withdrawal slip and gave it to the teller. She then checked my account and informed me that there was no money in my account. I must have had a startled strange look on my face, because she asked me if I was ok. I asked her to please check again and she for the second time stated there was no money. She further informed me that all the previous balance in the account of $4,500.00 had been withdrawn by my husband.

At that time, there were no cell phones or text messaging, so I had to wait until I saw him to get my husband's response. Somehow, I got through the day and I was anxiously waiting for my husband to provide some sort of explanation.

I called and asked my aunt if she would watch my kids that evening, and I spent some time with her, explaining why I didn't want my children at home that evening. It was late when I got home. I don't know what I was expecting, but I certainly wasn't expecting my husband to be soundly sleeping in bed as though everything was fine. My anger turned to rage at his peaceful appearance, and that's when I picked up the lamp.

I was shocked and frightened at my own rage. I walked and I cried, because I knew something was terribly wrong – wrong with my husband, wrong with me, and wrong with our marriage. After I had argued and talked with my hurt, confused self, the words to a hymn came into my head:

"We praise thee O God for the Son of thy love;
For Jesus who died and is now gone above.
Hallelujah thine the glory! Hallelujah Amen!
Hallelujah thine the glory! Revive us again."

Singing that praise hymn calmed me down and I was able to go back home and begin to face the ugly awfulness of my life. I didn't entertain the thought of killing my husband again, but I started to look for a way out of the marriage.

I deliberately got more involved in caring for my children, prayer, spending time involved in Bible study, and looking for a way out. These activities didn't change my circumstances overnight, but they started me on a journey that enabled me to maintain my sanity. I obtained the mental stamina to live each day and hope for a better future.

Chapter 2

Purpose and Process of Praise Therapy

The incident related in Chapter 1 took place 36 years ago when I made the discovery that my husband was a drug addict. The confrontation of his addiction was mentally, spiritually, and financially devastating for me and our children. I'm now aware that there are numerous families that face that reality today. It's amazing how the behavior of someone you love can change your life forever. I didn't know or understand about the devastation that drug addiction has on families until then. God knows I prayed and cried, supported my husband through rehabilitation, and did everything I knew how to do, but to no avail. In the end I just knew I couldn't let my life and the lives of my children be sacrificed on his altar of addiction.

I didn't turn to praise immediately. At first, I turned to running away, trying to deny my pain and problems, also trying to protect and insulate myself from getting my heart broken. The harder I tried to escape, the worse my life got. I learned the hard way that pain, problems, disappointment, and failure are a part of life that cannot be escaped. I had to face my own self and the way I was living.

Informed Consent

In all competent treatment practices, there is something called informed consent, meaning that ethically you are never asked to participate in something you don't understand or have not been informed fully about. Below is an explanation of *Praise Therapy.*

Praise Therapy is the application of biblical, spiritual mindfulness. *Praise Therapy* encourages the reader or participant to exalt, honor, and give glory to Elohim, Creator, God the Father of our Lord and Savior Jesus Christ, the eternal God of Abraham, Isaac, and Jacob.

> Psalm 21:13: *Be exalted, oh Lord, in Your own strength. We will sing and praise Your power.*

Seven things you should know about *Praise Therapy*:

1. *Praise Therapy* is not "religious;" it is relational and uses scriptures in the Bible.
2. *Praise Therapy* requires faith in the God of the Bible.
3. *Praise Therapy* is how you begin your day.
4. *Praise Therapy* is how you end each day.
5. *Praise Therapy* is ongoing. It requires self-examination and willingness to continue no matter what your life situation or circumstances.

6. *Praise Therapy* is a spiritual process that incorporates aspects of all the following evidenced based practices:
    - Acceptance and Commitment Therapy (ACT)
    - Cognitive Behavioral Therapy (CBT)
    - Compassion Focused Therapy (CFT)
    - Cognitive Processing Therapy (CPT)
    - Diabolical Behavioral Therapy (DBT)
    - Emotionally Focused Therapy (EFT)
    - Mindfulness Based Stress Reduction (MBSR)
    - Mindfulness Based Cognitive Therapy (MBCT)
    - Solution Focused Therapy (SFT)

7. *Praise Therapy* is a holistic approach that can be infused into your daily life as often as you find it necessary.

Chapter 3

Divine Mentality

All of *Praise Therapy* comes from a biblical perspective and that perspective is voiced by John in his letter to Gaius:

> 3 John 1:2: *Beloved, I pray that you may prosper in all things and be in health, just as your soul prospers.* (NKJV)

My experience with *Praise Therapy* came out of my desire to live out the salvation and grace that I have received. I will speak biblical truth as revealed to me from the Word of God, and the expected outcome is if you know the truth, the truth will make you free as well. I will be using words like sin, evil, wicked, satanic, and demonic, as these were/are the opposing spiritual powers or entities that are responsible for most of my mental and spiritual devastation–not other human beings.

> Ephesians 6:12 (NLT): *For we are not fighting against flesh-and-blood enemies, but against evil rulers and authorities of the unseen world, against mighty powers in this dark world, and against evil spirits in the heavenly places.*

Influenced by Fear

According to the Bible, anxiety, shame and depression come from a root of fear that is caused by mankind's disobedience to God. The disobedience is called SIN. According to my ancestors, 'there is no big or little sin; there is only sin.'

The original humans, Adam and Eve, both disobeyed and this caused them to become fearful, and then their fear disrupted their fellowship with God. Their immediate response was to cover themselves and hide from the presence of God. They experienced the first separation anxiety that resulted in spiritual death.

Like them, we also sin and our choices are now influenced by demonic forces over our soul-will or judgement, and this resulting influence is due to spiritual separation from God.

There was no fear, worry, shame, guilt, or death until there was disobedience. The act of disobedience separated me and you from God's perfect will, and will continue to do so if we don't take authority over it, and as an act of our will we choose to obey God. God gave us this power in the very first book of the Bible, Genesis. God has a conversation with Cain before he murders his brother Abel.

> Genesis 4:6-7 (NLT): *'Why are you so angry?' the LORD asked Cain. 'Why do you look so dejected? You will be accepted if you do what is right. But if you refuse to do what is right, then watch out! Sin is crouching at the door, eager to control you. But you must subdue it and be its master.'*

SIN is the problem. There is no person who is righteous, because all have sinned and come short of the glory of God.

That's why faith in Jesus the Christ is so important; He alone will save us from our sin (rebelliousness against God) and bring us into right standing with God. He was sacrificed. His blood was shed, and because of His obedience to the Father's perfect will, we now live in the dispensation of God's grace.

Influenced by the Grace of God

The miraculous grace of God enables those who believe in Jesus to have spiritual restoration with God and receive healing and deliverance from sin. This is called salvation!

> Romans 5:17 (NLT): *For the sin of this one man, Adam, caused death to rule over many. But even greater is God's wonderful grace and his gift of righteousness, for all who receive it will live in triumph over sin and death through this one man, Jesus Christ.*

Salvation is perfect redemptive power from God!

> Romans 1:16: *Therefore, we are not ashamed of the gospel of Jesus Christ, for it is the power of God unto salvation for everyone who believes.*

Everyone who believes they have received salvation is "SAVED." Jesus provided absolute salvation forever for me!

Past – I was saved from all my past sins.

Present – I am currently being saved from my confessed then repented sins.

Future – I will be saved from the eternal judgement of sin.

I praise God for His grace He provided through Christ Jesus. His grace healed my broken heart and restored my spiritual/physical/emotional/mental health. Due to His love and grace, I have a new perspective. My new perspective is a perspective of gratitude, joy, and praise!

"Praise Him! Praise Him!
Praise Him in the morning,
Praise Him in the noonday,
Praise Him when the sun goes down!"
(congregational praise song)

Chapter 4

Using Spiritual Mindfulness

Let the words of my mouth and the meditation of my heart be acceptable in Your sight.

Psalm 19:14

Praise Therapy uses spiritual (biblical) mindfulness, or what is commonly called meditation, to overcome and alleviate fear, anxiety, and depression from our lives. The application of spiritual mindfulness is what Joshua was instructed by God to do:

> Joshua 1:8 (NLT): *Study this book of instruction continually. Meditate on it day and night so you will be sure to obey everything written in it. Only then will you prosper and succeed in all you do.*

Praise Therapy is rooted in the instructions God gave to Joshua. By applying the principles in this book, you will gain the courage to face your life; not without problems, but while you are experiencing the problems, failure, difficulties, pain, and losses. Once you take on the daily practice of *Praise Therapy* you can expect a positive and more hopeful change in your mood, emotions, relationships, and life perspective.

God encouraged Joshua to continually focus on the instruction of His Word then apply it to his life every day.

This focus would give Joshua the courage and strength to help him succeed. And it will do the same for me and you. Meditating on God, who He is, what He has done, and what He will faithfully perform reassures our soul.

> Psalm 145:5 (NLT): *I will meditate on Your majestic, glorious splendor and Your wonderful miracles.*

Rejoice and Be Glad!

Over 35 times in scripture we are instructed to "rejoice and be glad." However, that's impossible to do unless we meditate on the goodness, mercy, and faithfulness of God. Rejoice means to delight and gladden yourself in God.

> Psalm 32:11 (NLT): *So, rejoice in the LORD and be glad, all you who obey him! Shout for joy, all you whose hearts are pure!*

Resetting Your Joy

Each day, due to life circumstances, we can find ourselves feeling discouraged, without joy, and despair can start to suck the hope and joy out of our lives. *Praise Therapy* is how I daily reach out and reset my joy. I think of this process as hitting the joy re-set button in my soul each day. I do this by addressing the worry or concern I have with the Word of God, then praising and praying my way through that circumstance.

Then, like Joshua, my meditation on the Lord will raise my level of mindfulness of who God is and what He has done. Then I can Re-joy! By focusing on the Lord. This mindset pleases God because it lets Him know I put my trust in Him.

> Philippians 4:4: *Always be full of joy in the Lord. I say it again—rejoice! (NLT)*
>
> Psalm 104:34: *May all my thoughts be pleasing to him, for I rejoice in the LORD.*
>
> Zephaniah 3:17: *For the LORD your God is living among you. He is a mighty savior. He will take delight in you with gladness. With his love, He will calm all your fears. He will rejoice over you with joyful songs.*

My Praise Has Nothing to Do with How I Feel

In all honesty, there are days when the last thing I want to do is rejoice. My mood is down, my situation appears to be out of control, and sometimes my sorrow or guilt about something is overwhelming. Added to these are my inner challenges of physical pain, and constant reminders in the news and personal reports from those I interact with that we live in a time of epidemic anxiety, depression, and despair everywhere.

A Godly man or woman can become depressed, but we don't stay there. I can personally relate to the depressed and anxious mood of many writers of the psalms and scriptures who often felt this way. Spiritually, our fear can take precedence over our thoughts and actions. When this happens, we find fault in everyone and everything. We blame our leadership, economy, and other people for our problems. Rarely do we want to take responsibility for the role we play. We prefer to ignore our sins, and in some cases, blame our sin on God. But David in the Bible didn't have this attitude. Although David was a king, he was also an adulterer, neglectful father, and murderer who confessed his sin and was honest with God. No matter how low David and other psalmists felt, they were always honest with God. For example, Psalm 51:2-6:

2 Wash me thoroughly from my iniquity,
And cleanse me from my sin.
3 For I acknowledge my transgressions,
And my sin is always before me.
4 Against You, You only, have I sinned,
And done this evil in Your sight—
That You may be found just when You speak,
And blameless when You judge.
5 Behold, I was brought forth in iniquity,
And in sin my mother conceived me.
6 Behold, You desire truth in the inward parts,
And in the hidden part You will make me to know wisdom.

As David confessed and repented, he talked to God, and when he was truthful and took his concerns and requests to God, he was spiritually able to recognize and honor the authentic heart and will of God. Psalm 51:6-9:

6 Behold, You desire truth in the inward parts,
And in the hidden part You will make me to know wisdom.
7 Purge me with hyssop, and I shall be clean;
Wash me, and I shall be whiter than snow.

[8] Make me hear joy and gladness,
That the bones You have broken may rejoice.
[9] Hide Your face from my sins,
And blot out all my iniquities.

Like David, when I practiced coming to God, I was able to make an exchange, a spiritual exchange, and that exchange caused a shift in David's prayer as he asked for the purity and righteousness of God to replace his sinful attitude and renew his fellowship with God.

My exchange brought about a major shift. The shift was from sin/self-consciousness – dwelling on the wrong I had done or the wrong that had been done to me – to God-consciousness – dwelling on the love and mercy of God. This shift caused David's prayer to end in praise and worship. Psalm 51:10-15:

[10] Create in me a clean heart, O God,
And renew a steadfast spirit within me.
[12] Restore to me the joy of Your salvation,
And uphold me by Your generous Spirit.
[14] Deliver me from the guilt of bloodshed, O God,
The God of my salvation,
And my tongue shall sing aloud of Your righteousness.
[15] O Lord, open my lips,
And my mouth shall show forth Your praise.

This exchange or spiritual mindfulness allows (me, us) to receive God's forgiveness and be spiritually renewed and restored. Then our mind is no longer anxious, down, or defeated because our spirit is lifted, invigorated, and inspired by the word of God. Through biblical mindfulness we gain the will to go on and persevere in life. Our hope is renewed, and we rejoice again. This is what I call *Praise Therapy*!

Chapter 5

Get Up and Praise God

This is the day the Lord has made I will ***rejoice*** *and be glad in it.*

Psalm 118:24

I woke up facing the despair of homelessness. For over an hour I just laid in bed, curled up in a knot with the covers pulled over my head, letting myself steep in the sadness of uncertainty. I didn't want to face this day! I already felt tired; my body ached with pain and my sense of failure was overwhelming. Yet despite what I felt like doing, I knew the day had to be faced. I prayed, "Lord please help me today." I allowed myself to just lose it, cry; and then somehow, I gained my composure and I thanked God for the strength to move forward. I got up out of my bed and kept packing.

The reality of knowing that I had to move out of my apartment by the end of the day had me feeling drained, defeated, and overwhelmed before I even started. Although I had asked for help from many resources, no one had responded to me. There was no one to help me. My children stood in front of me and I told them we were moving. I had to believe I would get what I needed to do done, and trust that my children would be alright.

> Psalm 73:26: *My flesh and my heart fail; But God is the strength of my heart and my portion forever.*

The confidence and peace that entered my heart, mind, and soul on that day is still present today. The Lord revealed to me who my greatest enemy really was...FEAR of what I didn't know and DOUBT of His ability to shepherd me through this valley that was only a *shadow of death.* That morning God revealed to me that FAITH and TRUST in Him were my greatest weapons, and the only defense that would be effective against losing my sanity.

> Psalm 55:22: *Give your burdens to the LORD and he will take care of you; he will not permit the godly to slip and fall. (NLT)*

> I Peter 5:7: *Give all your worries and cares to God for he cares about you. (NLT)*

Chapter 6

Praise Delivered Me out of Depression

I can't remember exactly when my faith became so strong that I started praising God to face my fears and overcome my anxiety and depression. I believe it was a gradual accumulation process that probably started on a morning two years prior to the morning I described in the previous chapter.

On this morning in the fall of 1987, I woke up terrified without any sense of peace or direction. I was terrorized by thoughts of failure, humiliated by my sin, and depressed with hopelessness that diminished my resolve as I faced the truth about my life circumstances. I was 38 years old, a divorced mother of 4 children, and recently abandoned by the man I had lived with for the previous 5 years. I foolishly, mistakenly thought I loved him and expected to marry him. I beat myself up, "You dumb stupid woman. What were you thinking? How could you allow yourself to get in this situation? Look at you, your life is a mess. How could you do this to yourself and your children?" There were so many accusatory thoughts in my head. Some of them were insane: "You should have just stayed where you were."

What made you think you could escape your empty, broke, and alone situation? I didn't know what to do. I was alone without help or support from anyone. Trembling, in tears I looked out of my kitchen window and focused on the top of Mt. Baldy. I stood there sobbing with tears flowing like a river and slinging snot for I don't know how long. I lost track of time. My children were in school, so it was safe for me to have a melt-down, to moan, sob, and cry out loud. I sat there moaning, with my heart crying out to God. I cried until the sobs were dry, and yelled until my throat was sore, "Dear God, help me!" There was no one to call. I knew there was no pill or drug to help me, because I needed more than alcohol to put me to sleep. I didn't just want to numb myself or experience an altered reality. I wanted my life to change. I wanted to be safe and secure (a competent person), have peace, know true love, and have a good life for me and my children.

I lost track of time and I don't remember how much time passed, so I just laid down, exhausted. I just laid down on the floor, a helpless, hopeless woman. Then there was a small voice that came from somewhere inside of me, "Hope in God; I will lift up my eyes to the hills from where my help comes from; the Lord, the maker of heaven and earth. When my heart is overwhelmed, lead me to the rock higher than I."

The voice inside of me was calming, comforting and reassuring. I stood up, leaned on the kitchen counter, and looked out of the window. Then the strangest thing happened. I started to praise and thank God that I had such a clear view of the mountain from my kitchen window, and a sense of peace and reassurance captured my soul. With that simple praise, I was able to focus on God and my anxiety quieted down.

I felt like God was asking me to trust Him and I gave God my desperation, hurt, pain, and fear. I looked up and focused on the mountain that was higher than my problems. As I lifted my thoughts in praise, I felt the weight of all the debt, despair, desertion, and hopelessness leaving me. My spirit grew lighter, and although I still didn't know how things were going to work out, in that moment I gained reassurance that they would. I felt 50 pounds lighter. A calm resolve came over my soul.

Psalm 62:5-8:

My soul, wait thou only upon God; for my expectation is from him. He only is my rock and my salvation: he is my defense; I shall not be moved.

In God is my salvation and my glory: the rock of my strength, and my refuge, is in God.
Trust in him at all times; ye people, pour out your heart before him: God is a refuge for us. Selah

Chapter 7

Praise Changed My Attitude from Despair to Hope

I realized a miracle had occurred and I shed my worry and fear that day. However, even after that experience of deliverance in my kitchen I knew that I needed help to deal with the anxiety and depression I was confronted with every day: the reality of going through the forced bankruptcy to applying for welfare and food stamps, all the while defending myself in labor board hearings and caring for the daily needs of my four children. I still found myself worrying about a lot of things. I didn't know who to talk to or how to ask for help. Although I went to church every week, I was closed off in my thoughts and feelings, and didn't feel like my emotions and mood were something my pastor or anyone else could help me with. I now understand that this was a symptom of my depression.

Pray for One Another

With the help and direction of the Holy Spirit I was empowered to attend early morning prayer at my church. I continued to cry out to God, and I appreciated the support of others as we prayed for one another. I went to early morning prayer for six months, Monday through Friday. I would get up at 4:30 a.m., shower, dress, and go to church at 5:30 a.m. to pray, come home at 6:30 a.m., wake up my kids, feed them breakfast, send them off to school, and I would spend my day studying the Bible, praying, looking for work, and volunteering at my church's drug and alcohol ministry. Every day I trusted and expected God to help me; to give me wisdom and direction, and He did.

"I love the Lord; He heard my cry."

I Got Radio Counseling

During this time, I also unexpectedly found support through Christian radio. I thank God for Charles Swindoll and his program, "Insight for Living." I had developed the habit of leaving the radio on and tuned to KSGN 24/7 at my home. I usually played the station music on a low volume day and night and would listen to certain programs.

I was listening to his radio broadcast one evening and he made a statement that he knew a lot of his listeners were going through some challenging times. He offered guidance through counseling to his radio audience. He said that if the listener would write a letter, his staff would answer and provide whatever feedback and support they could. So that evening I sat down and wrote to "Insight for Living." I wrote that I was reaching out for help and direction and I didn't know what to expect.

About a week later, I received a letter saying my letter had been received and I would be assigned to a counselor who would be in touch with me. A few weeks later I received another letter from a Dr. Barber, who shared that he had been forced into bankruptcy too, and although he hadn't been deserted by his partner, he understood how lonely it must be for me. He was very kind and nonjudgmental and said that their staff was praying for me. As we exchanged letters, I was able to tell my story and share my thoughts and fears openly with him.

After a month or so of writing, Dr. Barber called and encouraged me to keep praying and to trust God each day. He didn't offer any quick fix solutions, but he joined me in my faith and reassured me that God loved me and was concerned about me. From his encouragement I gained a deep internal certainty that I would live and not die. I remember it was a subtle, quiet, enduring experience as I used scripture from the Bible and applied them to my life.

As I studied and meditated on God's word, the fog of my defeated mentality lifted. I was able to cancel my ongoing pity party and receive the confidence I needed to commit to and pay attention to the needs of my children. I made a daily schedule and trusted God to order my steps.

By the time I wrote my last letter to Dr. Barber, the spirit of praise had permanently moved into my heart. I no longer saw myself as a victim, but I knew I had the victory.

Chapter 8

Praise Transformed My Mind and Mentality

I keep the telephone of my mind open to peace, harmony, health, love and abundance. Then, whenever doubt, anxiety, or fear try to call me, they keep getting a busy signal – and soon they'll forget my number.

Edith Armstrong

By focusing on the Lord in praise, the terrible weight of despair I felt arose and I began to hope again. I now realize that the word of God was transforming my mentality. According to Romans 12:1-3, my thoughts and feelings are being renewed by the transforming of my mind.

Faith in God served an eviction notice on the doubt, despair, and hopelessness that had formerly occupied my mind with racing thoughts of fear and dread. I knew that it was the power of the Holy Spirit that was transforming me spiritually and giving me the power to stand in hope.

As the power of the spirit of God infused my life, a miracle happened, and my reality became a different reality. I was not afraid anymore; I believed that despite my sin, poor decisions, and foolish mistakes, God's love for me was real and everlasting.

I would no longer give in to the sadness and sorrow of my life but would trust God and believe that I would overcome and succeed despite the obstacles I faced or the circumstances I was going through. Once I started praising and thanking God for being my provider and constant friend, I gained a deeper sense of reassurance that I would have the wisdom and strength to parent my children, gain understanding, help others, move out of poverty, and that my family would be safe.

John 6:63: *These words that I speak to you are spirit and life.* ~Jesus

Through praise I fell in love with Jesus again, like the words to "Falling in Love with Jesus," a favorite song by Jonathan Butler. In His arms I was protected; in His arms my mind was calmed. By reading, studying, and meditating on God's Word, I was able to sleep, and my spirit was comforted by His Word so that I could feel my anxiety and fear melting away.

Gradually, I stopped yelling at my kids and started to listen to them. Previously, I had only viewed them as responsibilities instead of my heritage of hope. I stopped being angry at my ex's, and accepted responsibility for the part I had played in my wrecked marriage and broken relationships. Most importantly, I chose to forgive because I had gained empathy for others and realized I needed forgiveness too.

As I forgave, I got healed from the rejection and pain of failed relationships and stopped looking for acceptance from a man to love and support me. I made up my mind to choose to praise and honor God.

An example of the praise that comes from faith in God and overcomes depression and anxiety is found in the book of Habakkuk 3:17-18:

> *Although the fig tree shall not blossom, neither shall fruit be in the vines; the labor of the olive shall fail, and the fields shall yield no meat; the flock shall be cut off from the fold, and there shall be no herd in the stalls: Yet I will rejoice in the LORD, I will joy in the God of my salvation.*

Benson commentary explains it this way:

> *Though all outward means of support should fail, yet will I* ***choose*** *to have a firm confidence in the power, goodness, and faithfulness of God, that he will preserve me, and supply me with all things necessary; and therefore, amidst the most threatening appearances of my life I will choose to praise Him, I will have inner peace and serenity of mind, because I trust in God.*

Trust must be demonstrated by waiting on the Lord! At first this was difficult for me. I remember wanting to go back and follow the man who had deserted me. I was so lonely and tired of doing everything for my children alone. I longed to have a relationship so badly, that I considered moving with my children to follow him to an unknown environment. I was struggling to decide.

I know it was the Holy Spirit who led me to use the wisdom of Esther in the Bible to help me make the right decision. I asked three seasoned intercessors to pray and fast with me while I sought the Lord for what to do. God's "NO" came loud and clear. I didn't follow the man but chose to trust God and **I got the victory over wanting to be with someone who didn't want to be with me**. I was also able to decide that I wouldn't be in a relationship until my children grew up and I would remain celibate until I got married again.

Strength to Begin Again

Making those decisions opened my life to greater clarity and understanding. I could see the possibilities for my life and the lives of my children. I was down, but I knew I wouldn't always live this way. I started back to college (after a 17-year gap) through the adult re-entry program at San Bernardino Valley College. The program was geared to adults like me who suffered from test anxiety, low self-esteem, and isolation. I started to hope again. I praised God for the combination of several part time jobs, Pell grants, and welfare, that helped me rebuild and sustain my family. After going to school full time for six years, while parenting and working, I graduated with a BA in Psychology and MA (MSW) in Social Work. It was nobody, but Jesus!

Chapter 9

Praise Therapy Is Spiritual Exercise for Your Soul

Exercise is a common activity for the physical body. We sit up. We push up. We lift weights up. All these exercise actions are directed upward against the down pull of gravity. The force of pushing and lifting against gravity makes our muscles stronger and our bodies powerful. With exercise we can build our physical strength and produce energy (power) to accomplish physical tasks. Another reward of physical exercise is that it improves your health and makes you stronger. The physical benefits of exercise strengthen muscle, burn fat, increase your circulation, raise your heart rate, and increase the flow of blood to your lungs and brain.

If you are out of shape physically, you are probably experiencing the negative effects of the lack of exercise. When you first begin to exercise you may feel like you will pass out because you can't get your breath, you start to sweat, and you experience cramps and pain in your muscles. But then if you continue to push your body through the unpleasant experience, a miracle or pleasant change starts to take place. With time, all the unpleasant symptoms fade or leave completely. You will find yourself experiencing a sense of wellbeing, euphoria, strength, and accomplishment. This is what *Praise Therapy* did for my soul and mentality.

Praise Therapy is a strength building exercise for your soul; it raises both your mental and spiritual resolve. What would happen if every time we felt fearful, confused, tired, weak, or emotionally drained, we took the time to praise God and thank Him for His goodness?

Depression makes you feel like you have a huge weight holding your spirit down. The constant downward pull of your thoughts, emotions, and feelings causes you to sink into isolation and darkness. The Bible describes it as a spirit of heaviness. I found out that *Praise Therapy* is using my faith in God's Word and the daily exercise of praise to raise or alter my emotions, thinking, and perceptions in order to do God's will. **It is always God's will to be praised!**

Using the Garment of Praise

Fear is a learned behavior, based on an experience or perception of something causing you harm. Fear, or the spirit of fear, is recognized as an evil spirit that is the cause of hatred, bitterness, despair, and hopelessness. You can't medicate fear. Fear must be faced with FAITH and your faith must be constantly fed and nourished for your spirit to be built up and strengthened by the Word of God.

My experience related in previous chapters is what many of us encounter when our spirit man is neglected through lack of spiritual exercise. We feel demoralized or rejected in some way. Our resolve, determination, and will to do better are constantly being attacked and pulled down by negative thoughts. *Praise Therapy* strengthens our minds through the power of God to choose rightly and wins against the assault of negative thoughts and self-talk. You've heard the expression "It's all in your head" but it is also in your spirit. A defeated spirit = A defeated mind.

The garment of praise is like a balloon that is filled with the breath and spirit of God to lift us. There is a power in the praise that removes the pain, encourages the soul, and strengthens the heart. The darkness runs, anger vanishes, and our peace is restored.

Psalm 42:5: *Why are you cast down within in me?*

When I neglect the spiritual exercise of praise, my soul gets weak, out of shape, and unable to perform at its highest level for my good. This makes me vulnerable to fear or becoming so hurt that I'm unable to learn from fear.

I understand the despair that can leave me so hopeless that I have thoughts of giving up and taking my life. It took the strong focus of faith in the Word of God to redirect my thoughts and actions. The strong focus I found was to meditate on scripture, pray, and find a way to use my interests and skills to step outside of my issues and help others. I found a good way to do this was to pray for others who might be suffering the same way I was. As I helped others, my depression and anxiety left.

Chapter 10

Cure for the Spirit of Heaviness

To console those who mourn in Zion, to give them beauty for ashes, the oil of joy for mourning, ***The garment of praise for the spirit of heaviness****; that they might be called trees of righteousness, the planting of the LORD, that He may be glorified.*

Isaiah 61:3 (NKJV)

Effects of a Spirit of Heaviness

There are times in everyone's life that the loss and devastation we experience can become overwhelming and seem too difficult if not impossible to bear. Our hearts are broken, and our souls are down cast. This spirit brings a "heaviness" over us:

- It dims our vision, robs us of our hope. We can only see the darkness.
- It brings a heavy, oppressive feeling. It quenches our faith.
- It may come over us at once, like a plague. It can be like a cloud, hanging over a place.
- It causes us to isolate, it steals our love, and makes us feel alone.

I consider the spirit of heaviness to be the same as depression. However, I've never heard depression referred to as a spirit in treatment. Depression is usually described as a mood disorder that can range from mild to severe in intensity and duration. The depression I experienced was situational and usually based on external circumstances that fostered thoughts and feelings of helplessness and hopelessness. I describe it as a mental weight of oppression.

Overthrowing the Spirit of Oppression

In the Bible, Jesus would cast out evil spirits and take authority over them. And He gave believers the power to do the same things He did.

> Luke 10:17: *'Lord, even the demons are subject to us in Your name.'*

Just like two objects can't occupy the same space at the same time, neither can two thoughts occupy your mind at the same time. I found that meditating on the Word of God and taking authority by praising God would elevate my thoughts and feelings so that the spirit of heaviness would leave me alone. I started to pay attention to my thoughts and mood.

First, I had to **R**ecognize the spirit of heaviness. I had to pay attention to my thoughts and feelings and put a limit on the amount of time I focused on negative and debilitating thoughts. I knew that I could cut it off, because as a child of God this was not God's will for me.

> Romans 8:31: *What shall we then say to these things? If God be for us, who can be against us?*

Then I had to actively **R**esist internalizing the spirit of heaviness. This meant I refused to believe (take in) thoughts that I would experience while under its influence. Finally, I **R**ejected self-critical, hateful thoughts, and attitudes about myself and others.

> 2 Corinthians 10:5: *We destroy arguments and every proud obstacle to the knowledge of God and take every thought captive to obey Christ.*

> Isaiah 61:3: *Put on the garment of praise.*

The only Rx prescribed in the Bible for the spirit of heaviness is the garment of praise. This literally means to be "wrapped up or covered in praise." Like physical clothing protects you from the outside atmosphere, God has given us the protective and comforting garment of praise to put on. To put on active praise means that every day you decide to spend time in worship that includes adoration, thanksgiving, singing, dancing, and glorifying God.

I defeated depression with praise! You can too! Get aggressive! Wrestle that oppressive spirit down. Read and meditate on Ephesians 6. Make God's praise glorious!

Chapter 11

Mindfulness Exercises

When I worked in rehabilitation programs, I learned about an acronym called HALT. The word halt means to stop. In former times this was a command given by guards to protect the security of a household or property. Their expression was "Halt! Who goes there?" Halt is a command we need to reflectively say to ourselves anytime we are experiencing anxious, depressed, or oppressed emotions that want to take over our peace and diminish our joy. The basis of "halt" is that we should never make decisions or trust our own thoughts if we are

1. **H**ungry,
2. **A**ngry,
3. **L**onely, or
4. **T**ired.

We should also always ask ourselves, "Who goes there?" or "What is going on with me?" This simple exercise in mindfulness can help you avoid many problems caused by worry and anxiety before they get out of control.

Face the Truth

Face the truth of what you are feeling and thinking. Find a counselor or someone to whom you can honestly say what your thoughts are, or journal and write your thoughts out. You can also draw a picture, play an instrument, do spoken word, or sing out your true feelings. Connect with yourself!

When we ignore or suppress our true feelings, or we don't pay attention, or we fear being shamed, we can become emotionally and spiritually anxious. When the problems of our anxious, depressed, or fearful thoughts aren't addressed, they create a distorted world of their own.

Examples of this can be seen in the comic characters of Schlep Rock from the Flintstones, Pig Pen from Charlie Brown, or Eeyore in Winnie the Pooh. These characters reflect their thoughts/feelings and experience a world separate from others or a break from the whole truth of their reality. Then they live out their false reality based on their experience, situation, or circumstances, which cause them to see, sense, and feel the world differently.

THINK

> Philippians 4:8 (NLT): *Fix your thoughts on what is true, and honorable, and right, and pure, and lovely, and admirable.* ***Think*** *about things that are excellent and worthy of praise.*

T = is it true?

H = is it helpful?

I = is it inspiring?

N = is it necessary?

K = is it kind?

Based on the above scripture I would deliberately focus on something that was praiseworthy whenever I started to get grumpy, complain, or make an excuse. My mental and emotional health grew stronger with this daily workout of praise. *Praise Therapy* was the workout for my soul and spirit; it motivated me and uplifted me to get up, look up, be up; it united me to be with Christ in heavenly places.

Praise Therapy combines both the practice of daily worship and daily meditation. For example, Psalm 103:1-6 (NIV):

> *Praise the LORD, my soul; all my inmost being, praise his holy name.*
>
> *Praise the LORD, my soul, and forget not all his benefits— who forgives all your sins and heals all your diseases, who redeems your life from the pit and crowns you with love and compassion,*
>
> *who satisfies your desires with good things so that your youth is renewed like the eagle's.*
>
> *The LORD works righteousness and justice for all the oppressed.*

This psalm is powerful to me when I think and meditate on all the things God has already done for me. This psalm also encourages me to praise God with everything in me and look carefully at the word – **ALL**. This psalm inspires, invigorates, and ignites my life. I start to count the benefits that God provides for me and my soul gets glad.

> Psalm 145:2: *Every day I will bless You, And I will praise Your name forever and ever.*

God's teaching, instruction and direction are only found in his word or the Bible. Only the Bible instructs and teaches us about the one true and living God who is always praiseworthy.

"*When I think of the goodness of Jesus*
and all that He's done for me,
my soul cries out Hallelujah!
Thank you, Lord for saving me."

OR

"*When I think about Jesus and what he's done for me. When I think about Jesus and how he's set me free. I could dance, dance, dance, dance, dance, dance, dance all night!*"

(congregational praise lyrics)

Chapter 12

Praise Therapy Defeated Anxiety

Isaiah 26:3, 4

(NASB): *The steadfast of mind You will keep in perfect peace because he trusts in You.*

(KJV): *Thou wilt keep him in perfect peace whose mind is stayed on Thee because he trusted in thee.*

When *Praise Therapy* began, I didn't know it was therapy. I just knew I had to do something to maintain my sanity each day. I needed the mental strength to stay focused and keep me and my children alive. I had no telephone and even if I had one there was no one to call. God had my full attention.

> Psalm 46:1: *God is my refuge! He is my strength! He's a very present help in the time of trouble.*

I turned to God in earnest trust and recited and meditated on Philippians 4:6 (NLT):

> *Don't worry about anything; instead pray about everything. Tell God what you need and thank him for all He has done!*

I would read the Bible every day. I made an appointment to have a designated time with God in His word every morning. Anyone who needed to get into the bathroom during that time just had to wait. I started to personalize scripture and put my name or first personal pronoun into each one of the scriptures that I wanted to apply to my life. For example:

> Psalm 91:1: *I dwell in the secret place of the most high God. I shall abide under the shadow of the Almighty.*
>
> Philippians 4:19: *I can do all things through Christ who strengthens me.*
>
> Psalm 27:1: *The Lord is my light and my salvation who shall I fear? The Lord is the strength of my life, of whom will I be afraid?*

Next, when I prayed, I started by praising God first instead of just asking for what I wanted. For example:

- I praise You Lord, because Your mercies are new every morning.
- I praise You Lord, because of Your faithfulness and loving kindness.
- I praise You Lord for Your daily provision and protection; for preparing a table before me in the presence of my enemies.
- I praise You for Your love and the redemptive power of Your blood.
- I praise You for Your gift of salvation and forgiveness in Christ Jesus
- I praise You for Your grace and favor over my life.
- I praise You because even though sin may abound Your grace abounds much more.

Singing Songs and Making Melody in My Heart

I would sing hymns or gospel songs all day long and memorize each verse. For example, I'm probably the only person who knows all 5 verses of "Amazing Grace;" "It is Well with My Soul;" "I Need Thee Every Hour;" or "I Trust in God." These are older church hymns, but they would encourage my heart and built me up spiritually.

It's in memory of women like my grandmother, Jessie Louise White Tyus, who had a very hard life as the oldest of 16 children. She was expected to care for her younger sisters and brother after the death of her mother, Mary Walker White, when she was eight years old. My great-grandfather married again and had 12 more children by his second wife, Lelia. She also died and my grandmother raised her younger siblings as her own. My grandmother married Charles Tyus and had four children of her own. Due to mysterious circumstances, she had to flee the south and move to California in 1929. The belief is that Charles killed or harmed a white man.

My grandmother experienced the death of her two oldest sons; one died in Tennessee en route to California, and another, shortly after they arrived. She never saw her first siblings again. She couldn't even write to them for fear of being found. My grandmother had her share of disappointment, sorrow, hurt, and pain. Although she could read and write, and was a talented seamstress, she worked as a maid all her life. As a young child I heard her sing. I saw her shout and clap herself happy. I didn't understand what she was doing then but now I believe I was witnessing *Praise Therapy* in action.

God would put a song of praise in my heart and my mouth all during the day. However, the most powerful part of the therapy was that I would sing scripture. I learned that there were tunes for a lot of scriptures and I also made up some of my own.

> Psalm 27: *The Lord is my light and My Salvation; whom shall, I fear? The Lord is the strength of my life; of whom shall I be afraid?*
>
> Psalm 3: *Lord, how they increase that trouble me; many are they who rise up against me. Many are they that say of my soul there is no help for her in God, but You O Lord are a shield for me, my glory and the lifter of my head.*
>
> Psalm 5: *Give ear to my words. O Lord, consider my meditation, listen to my cry for help, my King and my God. For unto You will I pray. My voice will You hear in the morning; O Lord in the morning will I direct my prayer to You and I will look up.*
>
> Psalm 25: *Unto You O Lord do I lift up my soul. O my God I trust in You. Let me not be ashamed; let not my enemies' triumph over me.*

Singing the word of God out loud and to myself calmed and regulated my thoughts and emotions.

Chapter 13

Decreeing and Declaring Faith

I know what it's like to fight for my sanity, to face loneliness, poverty, rejection, shame, and grief. I know how your mind can be so tormented with negative thoughts of failure, and overwhelmed with persecution to the point where there seems to be no way out.

Today I praise God because I was blessed to take my wounded, battered, brokenness to Him. God never rejected me, and His spirit gave me hope that I would succeed! The process of *Praise Therapy* taught me to speak the word of God over my life by decreeing and declaring the desires of my heart into every situation.

Decreeing and Declaring Are a Spiritual Principal!

> Job 22:28 NKJV: *You will also declare a thing, and it will be established for you; so light will shine on your ways.*

This scripture reinforces what my mother used to say, "Be careful what you say, because you may have to eat those words." There is power in the words we say and speak over our lives. Declaring God's praises changed the lens through which I saw my own life. As I started to apply *Praise Therapy*, I thought more about what I would say before I spoke.

Psalm 19:14: ***Let the words of my mouth, and the meditation of my heart****, be acceptable in Your sight, O LORD, my strength, and my redeemer.*

I made daily decrees and declarations through affirmations over my life each day that reflected my faith and not my thoughts.

Speaking OUT LOUD to myself, I declared:

Jesus is Lord over my life, the lives of my children, and all that concerns me! I will do what pleases God!! I will not take drugs or sell drugs; I will not sell my body for prostitution. I will not lie, cheat, or steal. I will not ever again be in a relationship just to have a man in my life. I will only fulfill my sexual desires in a committed, loving marriage.

I also decreed and declared:

My children will not take drugs, they will not be gang members, and they will resist gang mentality and culture.

I also decreed and declared:

My children will complete school and will have excellent education and training.

I further decreed and declared:

No spirit will rule over our lives except the Spirit of the true and living God, the Father of my Lord and Savior Jesus Christ.

I continue to decree and declare:

Each of our lives will fulfill God's purpose for us and all our lives will bring God glory and honor.

Many times, I've asked myself why I didn't just give in or accept what I saw all around me? I now know and understand that it was the power and presence of God that came into my life through praise. Praise empowered me to have confidence and not give in to my worry, fears and depression.

Chapter 14

Praise Is a Choice

I will lift my eyes to the hills from whence cometh my help.

Psalm 121:1

No one can force you to praise God. It must be done of your own free will. All I can tell you is that when I made the choice to praise God, I saw and personally experienced my thoughts go from suicidal and destructive to joyful and glad. I've experienced moving from a time when I didn't know how to love, forgive, or have gratitude to be a person who can give and receive love without fear, forgive with compassion, and be truly thankful.

This change happened over the years as I always made the mindful choice to bless the Lord, and that His praise would continuously be in my mouth (see Psalm 34:1-3). This attitude has kept my mind and emotions stable and resilient through the worst situations in my life:

- Being homeless, living in a gang-infested neighborhood
- Experiencing break-ins and robbery
- Witnessing murders, police brutality, and mayhem
- Experiencing drug, sexual, and emotional abuse

I could continue to give you my examples, but instead I challenge you to insert your own trauma, hurt, pain, disappointment, and suffering. Then apply *Praise Therapy* to it.

A Conscious Choice

Praising God is a conscious choice that I made despite what I saw, felt, or thought in the natural. I am the first to admit that praising God is not always easy, but it is always a choice. The choice to praise God is always available. Nothing and no one can take that from me. Every day I have the choice to either believe God and praise Him for new mercies each morning and His faithfulness each night, or I can choose to hold onto yesterday's fears and insecurities, believe a lie, depend on my own weak efforts, and sink downward into despair.

Where Does the Relationship of Faith Choice Come From?

In the Bible, Abraham is our spiritual father of faith. According to scripture, it was Abraham's faith in God (not the keeping of the law) that produced righteousness.

> Genesis 15:6: *Abraham believed God and it was counted to him as righteousness.*

Using *Praise Therapy,* I can make the same choice Abraham made to believe God. When I choose to praise God, I join generations of people of faith who listened to God, believed God, and trusted God. They are described in the book of Hebrews as a great cloud of witnesses. You can also choose to make this choice.

The praise I choose to give is not based on or related to the situation or circumstances of my life, although praise to God is most often associated with only the receiving of good and then blaming God when terrible things happen.

> Job 2:9-10: *Then Job's wife said to him, 'Do you still retain your integrity? Curse God and die!' 'You speak as a foolish woman speaks,' he told her. 'Should we accept from God only good and not adversity?' In all this, Job did not sin in what he said.*

In contrast, there is a sacrifice of praise, that is made while you are in a dark place, you don't have the answer, but you trust that God does.

> Hebrews 13:15: *Therefore, through Him (Jesus) let us continually offer up to God a sacrifice of praise, that is, the fruit of our lips that confess His name.*

This choice to praise while in pain, while enduring suffering, or while you are grieving comes from faith and trust in a God who is greater than your circumstances. Praise puts your focus above all the death, despair, and destruction that may be surrounding you. *Praise Therapy* lifts your eyes, mind, and countenance upward to God. My praise must come from faith – what I/you intrinsically believe about God, more than myself/yourself, or the circumstances of the world I live in.

> *"You don't get in life what you want, you get what you believe."* Oprah Winfrey

Perfect Peace Over Anxiety

When you make the choice to believe God, He promises to keep you in "perfect peace." (see Isaiah 26:3, 4. That perfect peace is the peace God gives because I've put my trust confidence in Him.

1 Peter 5:7: *Casting our cares on God, because he cares for us.*

This applies not only to natural provision of food, clothing, and shelter, but to the spiritual provision of peace, mercy, and love. Jesus has said, "I will never leave you or forsake you.

Chapter 15

Praise Is a Chief Weapon of Spiritual Warfare

I will call upon the Lord who is worthy to be praised and so shall I be saved from my enemies.

Psalm 18:3

Fighting for your sanity and dignity, while at the same time struggling to make right choices is mental and spiritual warfare. Following are three examples of how praise was used by the nation of Israel to gain victory in their battles against overwhelming odds.

- Moses lifted his hands; the armies prevailed.
- The walls of Jericho fell with a loud shout of praise.
- The armies of Judah won the battle against not one, but three opposing armies without ever lifting a sword or shooting an arrow, because the armies were led by worship and praise!

2 Chronicles 20:21 NLT: *After consulting the people, Jehoshaphat appointed men to sing to the LORD and to praise him for the splendor of his holiness as they went out at the head of the army, saying: "Give thanks to the LORD, for his love endures forever."*

In these examples there is a clear indication that praise prevails over real life problems. In the spiritual atmosphere praise takes authority over every circumstance in your life and allows you to align yourself with the authority and power of God to fight for you.

As a single African-American mother of four children, I experienced the daily warfare and remember the constant fear and apprehension I felt for the safety and lives of my children. Knowing that no matter how well I raised them, there were all kinds of enemies, dangers, evil people out there, and wicked circumstances to corrupt, confuse, cause harm, and take the lives of my children.

This concern was a constant and real threat, and my dilemma was how not to be over-vigilant, let them learn from the natural consequences of their behaviors, not become angry and bitter at the injustice displayed toward them, but to teach them about righteousness, even when they might not be treated fairly. This was especially true for my sons, whom I had to teach that they could lose their lives just for being Black. Even if they made an honest mistake, I knew that many times Black children were not allowed to learn from their mistakes, but were only punished for them.

> Romans 12:21: *Don't be overcome by evil but overcome evil by doing good.* (NIV)

When you are engaged in warfare it's important to know whose side you are fighting for and which side you are fighting against. So even though wrong may be done to me and my family I had to understand that I was not to return evil for evil. I must be clear that my warfare is against evil! Yes, I acknowledge that racism is evil and wrong, but when I fight against it according to my own evil thoughts and desires, then I am a part of the same evil that I hate.

The same principle applies to economic injustice. It's wrong and evil to oppress the poor. Poverty is difficult to live in, but I also knew that I would have to trust God to provide the money and resources I needed. God promised to provide my daily bread or needs. Jesus is Lord of my life. Therefore, I wouldn't sell my soul by stealing from others or becoming a workaholic to the neglect of my family and health to get my needs met. Praising God allowed me to escape the satanic delusion that I was the one who was responsible for my own life and provision.

Chapter 16

Praise Is a Spiritual Weapon

The warfare is never physical, but a spiritual battle that must be fought with spiritual weapons.

> 2 Corinthians 10:4: *The weapons of our warfare are not carnal, but spiritual and mighty unto God to the tearing down of strong holds.*

Here is one testimony of God's provision for me and my children: During the recession of the 80's economic shut down, there were no jobs. Major industries like steel mills like US Steel, Kaiser, and the supporting industries that were a part of their production had closed. Union jobs that paid livable wages and had benefits were replaced with service jobs that paid minimum wage and no benefits. I was an operating engineer, but there were no construction jobs available unless I wanted to go to Saudi Arabia or Venezuela. There would be hundreds of applications for one position, and even though I had always worked, I found myself working low wage part-time jobs, on unemployment, and using food stamps to feed my children. No matter how I stretched and budgeted, I would always run out of food and money by the 25th of the month. The system was designed this way to build fear and "decrease dependence." Well there are few pains like the worry and frustration of not having enough food to feed your children. Although I had the means and skills to do things illegally, after God delivered me, I had made up my mind that I wasn't going to steal, prostitute, or sell drugs to make money.

The Bible says, "Bring your tithes into my storehouse," so I started tithing (giving the first 10th of my income) on what I had, which was food stamps and money from recycling and volunteering my time. After two years, my unemployment benefits had run out. If you have ever been on welfare, you know that there is just enough coming in to keep you alive and place you in the vicious cycle of the 1st and the 15th, but I kept praying and giving what I had, and God kept giving us our daily bread. During that time, I worked fast food at Taco Bell, drove a truck for Goodwill industries, and did janitorial work in the administration building at Norton AFB. Thankfully, I got permission at Norton to salvage the computer paper and aluminum cans. This money paid for gas to get to work, toiletries, soap, toilet paper, and detergent. I budgeted everything.

I remember praising God that my health was good and thanking Him for protecting the lives of me and my children. Miracles started to take place. My children didn't get sick, so we didn't need health insurance. A young couple from my church said that God had put me on their hearts so that when they went grocery shopping, they would buy food for me. Others would keep me informed of government food distributions, and still others would help me out of the surplus of their pantries so that we had food to eat.

Another miracle was that my children learned to shop at secondhand stores. Of course, at first, they didn't like it, but our reality was that when school started I had only $100.00 to spend on four children for school clothes. I challenged my children to get five outfits for their 25.00. The blessing was that my children learned to stretch a dollar and looked for coupons for everything.

The largest miracle I experienced was being gifted the condo/apartment that we lived in. Yes, my landlord, a young Asian man, not even a Christian, gave me a house. He called me one morning and asked me if I wanted to own the apartment I was living in. At first, I hesitated because I was on welfare and only working part time, but then he asked me again and explained that if I didn't want it, he would give it to his sister. I said yes. I woke up that morning renting, and I went to bed that night owning the property. The loan was assumable, and it cost me $250.00 to get the title changed to my name. God is a promise keeper!

Actively praising God gave me the determination to stand against anxiety, even though there were awful uncertain situations around me. I was determined not to be anxious or to worry, even though I may not have had everything I needed now. My determination was not to be afraid, even though I was in some frightening situations. I was able to ball up my fist, strengthen myself in the Lord, and fight the good fight of faith. I continued to decree and declare that my children and I would come out of this situation and have the favor of the Lord.

Christ's triumph over sin on the cross and his victory over death through his resurrection made *Praise Therapy* possible. How?

> Galatians 2:21: *I am crucified with Christ, nevertheless I live, yet not I, but Christ lives in me, and the life I now live in the flesh I live by faith in the Son of God who loved me and gave himself for me.*

As I trusted in Jesus and believed His Word, every day my heart and mind were transformed, and I exchanged the anxiety and worry for trust and security that comes only from the Word of God.

Chapter 17

My Life Was Transformed Through Praise

Through meditating on the word of God I was renewed by the transforming of my heart and mind.

> Romans 12:1 (NLT): *Don't copy the behavior and customs of this world, but let God transform you into a new person by changing the way you think. Then you will learn to know God's will for you, which is good and pleasing and perfect.*
>
> Philippians 4:6: *Be anxious for nothing, but in everything with prayer and supplication make your request known to God.*

The bottom line is either I trust God, or I don't. I discovered that whenever I was overwhelmed with worry and fear, I was trusting in myself or another person to have the solution, rather than trusting God. When I began to praise God and meditate on His Word, I gained the ability to face and confront my anxious, depressive, and fearful thoughts, then counter those thoughts and feelings with the word of God.

Praise Positively Changed My Parenting

A big challenge for me was parenting my four children being on welfare, while working part time and going to school full time. Many days I had to leave my children and trust that they would be safe until I saw them again in the evening. I prayed over my children each day. Daily praise increased the love I have for my children and I saw them as the blessing they were meant to be in my life. I could relate to my children in love and better understand their needs, whereas before, I was distracted and only into my own pain. Now, I could see their hurt, confusion, and pain that I had caused by my previous neglect of them. I was so thankful for the compassion God had shown me. Through His love I was able to humble myself before my children. I apologized to them and asked for their forgiveness and I changed how I disciplined and corrected them. For example, when I felt tempted to lose my temper and unleash my anger:

> Psalm 4:4: *Don't sin by letting anger control you. Think about it overnight and remain silent.*
>
> Ephesians 4:26: *Don't sin by letting anger control you. Don't let the sun go down while you are still angry.*

Praise Positively Changed My Attitude

Parenting was not the only area that changed; through praise my entire thought life was transformed. I couldn't think and act like I formerly had; everything in me went before God in praise.

For example, when I was tempted to gratify a grudge, gossip, over eat, tell a lie, or not forgive, I would hear God's word admonishing me:

> Romans 6:12 (KJV): *Let not sin therefore reign in your mortal body, that ye should obey it in the lusts thereof.*

> Romans 6:12-14 (NLT): *Do not let sin control the way you live; do not give in to sinful desires. Do not let any part of your body become an instrument of evil to serve sin. Instead, give yourselves completely to God, for you were dead, but now you have new life. So, use your whole body as an instrument to do what is right for the glory of God. Sin is no longer your master, for you no longer live under the requirements of the law. Instead, you live under the freedom of God's grace.*

A huge area for me was to make peace with my sexuality. Due to the sexual abuse I had experienced as a young child, my sexuality had been perverted. And although I had been married and was the mother of 4 children, I needed to think differently about sexual gratification, present my body to God, live a celibate life, and allow His Spirit to restore the right thoughts, affections, and desires within me.

> 1 Thessalonians 4:3-5: *God's will is for you to be holy, so stay away from all sexual sin. Then each of you will control his own body and live in holiness and honor— not in lustful passion like the pagans who do not know God and his ways.*

It is against God's will for me to have sexual intimacy outside of marriage. The penal code describes rape as a sexual physical assault without consent or against a person's will. Since the spirit of God dwells in me as a believer, then when I engage in sex unmarried, it is against the will of God. Therefore, in order to please God, I must obey Him according to His will and conform my will to His, not the other way around. This principle is difficult for most sexually mature adults to follow and understand because we don't realize that sexual intimacy is more than a physical act; it is also spiritual.

I now see my sexuality as part of my praise! How I glorify God with my body. Therefore, according to scripture, I will only allow my body to have sexual intimacy in marriage, and if my body tries to do otherwise, I need to take authority over my will, to the point of commanding my body to conform to the will of God.

My mental focus and emotional health grew stronger with the daily workout of praise and meditation. *Praise Therapy* at the beginning, during, and end of my day motivated me and uplifted me to Get Up, Look Up, and Be Up for whatever I had to face each day. *Praise Therapy* focused my mind on the love that Christ has for me, the love I have for Him, and transformed the love I have for myself and others.

Chapter 18

Praise Each Day Will Keep Stress Away

I'm grateful for the leading and guiding of the Holy Spirit. Although I still have some days when I can sink into despair, I must force myself to intentionally focus on God and praise Him! I've learned that just because an opportunity presents itself for me to be anxious or depressed, I don't have to take it! I don't have to live crazy or be emotionally unstable.

Sometimes, I still get thoughts or feelings of doubt, and wonder if I have achieved any accomplishments because of praise. However, the truth is all that I have achieved in maintaining a healthy life approach is the result of replacing my anxious, depressed, and fearful thoughts with praise. So, I now step out with sharing my journey and encouraging others to praise God through every situation and circumstance.

We currently live in a time of epidemic depression, anger, anxiety, and fear that feed into the catastrophic rate of drug addiction, suicide, and murder. It is my hope that *Praise Therapy* will help alleviate these symptoms in others as it has done for me. Our human struggles are difficult, but *Praise Therapy* offers a solution that heals the spirit and gives one the redetermination to see life differently. Then it incorporates spiritual support as a part of a healthy living style.

Let Everything That Has Breath Praise the Lord!

I have used *Praise Therapy* as a spiritual form of stress relief for over 30 years. It has produced positive enduring benefits for my life. Today, there are few if any problems that move me into high stress, despair, or loss of hope.

I know I have a friend in Jesus! What a friend I have in Jesus, all my sins and griefs to bear. Jesus is all the world to me: my life, my hope, my all. He is my strength from day to day; without Him I would fail. Following Him I know I'm right; He watches over me day and night. He's my friend!

When there was no money, no job, or other monetary support, I used *Praise Therapy* to decrease and relieve me of anxious and fearful thoughts. I have used *Praise Therapy* while addressing severe illness, loneliness, mental distress, and despair. In my experience, I have used *Praise Therapy* as a holistic approach that promotes my overall wellbeing without compromising my health or the wellbeing and safety of others.

Praise Honors God and God Honors Praise

This is how praise honors God:

- Through our spirit (the life force that comes from God)
- Through our soul (beliefs, thoughts, emotions, will, and perceptions resulting from learning and experience)
- Through our body (our unique physicality)

Praise brings our life force (spirit), our thoughts and beliefs (soul), and our physical body into the presence of God. That's where the blessings of abundance and fulness are found.

In His presence:

Psalm 16:11 (NLT): *You will show me the way of life, granting me the joy of Your presence and the pleasures of living with You forever.*

Praise joins your thoughts with the mind of Christ:

Philippians 2:5: *Let this mind be in you which was also in Christ Jesus.*

Praise joins your body to the fellowship of true worship in heaven:

Revelation 5:13: *Blessing and honor and glory and power belong to the one sitting on the throne and to the Lamb, forever and ever.*

Praise puts God first in your life then His Spirit (Word) will rule over your soul (will, thoughts, feelings, and emotions). He won't take your choice from you, but because you love Him you always want your choices to please Him. Paul taught that it is the love of Christ that constrains us in our behavior. Our love and submission to His will is how we demonstrate that we love God.

Praise Will Help You Commit Your Way to God!

In one year, I suffered the loss of my business (forced into bankruptcy), the loss of my home (foreclosure), desertion (the man partner left), the death of my brother, and the death of my father, all while suffering the loss of mobility due to back and sciatica nerve pain.

My overwhelming sense of loss and being unable to control the outcomes of the pain, death, and dying I was experiencing sent my emotions on a hurricane roller coaster ride. Being torn from those you love through death can't be described in words. I'm so glad that with each occurrence of death God gave me the courage and resolve to go on.

We all go through emotionally difficult times. When tragic loss occurs, it probably is the hardest part of our human experience. In my case, it was back-to-back unrelenting sadness and sorrow. Yet, I was not praising God for the loss or situation I was in. I praised Him for sustaining me through it all. I held on to the solid Rock of Christ Jesus, knowing I had the responsibility of my children, I wanted to live for them. I had to make up my mind and choose to praise. My declaration was "Lord, I choose to praise and trust in You, no matter what I'm going through!"

I walked, crawled and sometimes just laid down in my faith. I found out that the grief experience was something that I would come out of, but not by trying to escape from it or denying the pain and despair of it. Miraculously, like the Hebrew boys during the fiery furnace, and like Paul and Silas in prison, with prayer and praise I came through my grief and loss stronger than when I started.

My prayer: Lord, I love You and I come to You because although my heart is overwhelmed with grief, depression, and pain, I choose to praise and put my trust in You. I know that somehow You will bring me out of this. You will cause me to know joy and laughter again. I believe that You will make ALL THINGS work together for my good. Amen!

Chapter 19

Praise Is Our Highest Expression of Worship

You are worthy, our Lord and God, to receive glory and honor and power, for You created all things, and by Your will they were created and have their being.

Revelation 4:11

Praise is the highest expression of worship! Praise of the true and living God is always done in spirit and in truth. When the Apostle John saw the throne room in heaven there was continual praise there.

"*Every praise is to our God!*" Hezekiah Walker

One of the limitations of the English language is that we don't understand or fully appreciate the meaning of the word "praise" in its full context. We are familiar with giving praise for something that is good, or something we like, or behavior we approve of. However, in the Hebrew and Aramaic languages, praise also involves the essence of integrity, in one's character. This means that we praise God for who He is, not only for what He does. Praise indicates that we worship God and fully put our trust in Him.

"*Because of who You are I give You glory; because of who You are I give You praise.*" Martha Munizzi

In the context of *Praise Therapy*, glory is given to God for who He is in His sovereign authority as Omniscient (all knowing), Omnipresent (all existing), Omnipotent (all powerful) God. Glory is given for His divine attributes. Praise is the tangible essence of faith in my life. Praise makes it possible for me to "faith my way through" all of life's challenging situations. I will have valleys in my life; there will be dark shadows, and the finality of death will come. Death, though difficult to accept and painful to experience, will always be the end of our physical life.

Jesus told His disciples not to rejoice that they had power over the evil one, as important as that is, but rather to rejoice that their names were written in the book of life.

> Luke 10:20 (NLT): *But don't rejoice because evil spirits obey you; rejoice because your names are registered in heaven.*

That's why I praise God! Because I have eternal life! Jesus has promised that He will always be with us. "My spirit will always be with you," He said. All the praise that I offer is based on God's Word and what He has revealed to us about His divine and eternal attributes.

Praise and Prayer are Sacred to God!

From my experience I've learned that praise and prayer are both sacred offerings to God. That's why there are so many attacks and attempts to smother praise and silence prayer. Truly there is no greater evidence of a sovereign, merciful, loving and just God than the ability to praise Him and pray to Him. Through prayer we can communicate with God and God wants us to talk to and listen to Him. We are always to pray, but often prayer is used as the last resort–what we do when we are desperate and have tried everything else. This approach gives the impression that prayer is just the emergency cord we pull in a crisis after all our efforts have failed.

Similarly. praise is often separated even further and placed in a "sacred" place for worship only. This means it is limited to the space of a sanctuary in a church or cathedral, only in a congregation or worship service. Recently, a common expression I've heard is "I'm going to church to get my praise on" or "I can't wait to get to praise and worship." These expressions make it appear as though praise of God is limited to designated worship services on Saturday or Sunday morning. However, this is not the truth or God's desire for us. God wants to continually be worshipped; His praise is to be continuous, nonstop! All the time! In every one of us!

> Psalms 149:6 *Let the praises of God be in their mouths, and a sharp sword in their hands.* (NIV)

Chapter 20

Praise Is a Faith Activator

Jesus left us an endowment of praise and prayer. The Lord's Prayer, which is a model prayer that is prayed all over the world in every language, begins and ends with praise!

> Matthew 6:9-14: *Our Father in heaven, Hallowed be Your name.*
>
> *Your kingdom come. Your will be done on earth as it is in heaven.*
>
> *Give us this day our daily bread.*
>
> *And forgive us our debts, as we forgive our debtors.*
>
> *And do not lead us into temptation but deliver us from the evil one. For Yours is the kingdom and the power and the glory forever. Amen.*

Praise gives me the courage and strength to walk in the spirit. Praise activates my faith to believe God. Praise disciplines my mind and exalts my spiritual nature over my physical flesh and life circumstances. That's why Nehemiah could proclaim that the joy of the Lord was his strength and Job could proclaim, blessed be the name of the Lord, or James could count it all joy! Lord, I will praise You according to Your Word, according to Your divine attributes.

Scripture Affirmations

The following affirmations come directly from the Bible.

- ❖ Lord I praise You because according to Your Word this is the day that You have made. I will rejoice and be glad in it.
- ❖ Lord I praise You because according to Your Word I am fearfully and wonderfully made.
- ❖ Lord I praise You because according to Your Word You have not given me the spirit of fear but Your spirit of peace, love, and a sound mind.
- ❖ Lord I praise You because according to Your Word You are my light and my salvation.
- ❖ Lord I praise You because according to Your Word You are my shepherd and I shall not want.
- ❖ Lord I praise You because according to Your Word NOTHING can separate me from Your love.
- ❖ Lord I praise You because according to Your Word You will never leave me or forsake me.
- ❖ Lord I praise You because according to Your Word all things are working together for my good.

- Lord I praise You because according to Your Word You can do exceedingly, abundantly, above all that I ask or think, according to the power that works in me.

- Lord I praise You because according to Your Word You will keep me in perfect peace, if I will focus on and trust in You.

- Lord I praise You because according to Your Word You love me with an everlasting love.

- Lord I praise You because according to Your Word all my children will be taught by Your Spirit.

- Lord I praise You because according to Your Word my children are a heritage and blessing from You.

- Lord I praise You because according to Your word You will fight for me and protect me from my enemies.

The opportunities to praise God from His Word are endless! His Word is Spirit and Truth!

"I lift my hands in total praise to You!"
Richard Smallwood

I have discovered that it is impossible to honestly lift praise to God and worry at the same time! I will repeat it again for emphasis: **It is impossible to praise God and worry at the same time!** Worry (and all the things that come with it – anxiety, depression, fear, and emotional pain) and praise are mutually exclusive activities. **You can't participate in both at the same time.**

In Matthew Chapter 6, Jesus told His followers to "take no thought" for things like food and shelter. He was saying, "Don't worry; don't be fearful." He asked them, "Can all your worries add a single moment to your life?" Likewise, you can ask yourself, "Has worrying ever accomplished anything for me?"

> *"Worry never robs tomorrow of its sorrow; it only saps today of its joy."* Leo Buscaglia

Worry wears us down. Praise lifts us up. Worry embodies Satan's will, while praise of God enthrones Him in our circumstances! Remember, whatever comes to kill, steal, or destroy your love, joy, or peace is an attack from the enemy against your faith. The attacks will come; they are unavoidable! We live in a fallen world where death, disappointment, discouragement, and despair are all around us, but as you become skilled in using *Praise Therapy*, your praise will break the back of Satan's attacks! You will find that you have the strength to resist mental and emotional anguish and you will be less anxious, fearful, and depressed.

The Bible tells us not to worry 365 times! That's a warning from God's Word for every day of the year! DO NOT WORRY! This means don't be anxious, fearful, or afraid of anything. By God's grace we are empowered to make the choice to praise Him every day.

I am so thankful that God's love reached out to me and gave me the grace and ability to praise Him! I pray that the next time you are tested, and the trials of life seem insurmountable, or even if your day is free of problems and concerns, that you make the volitional choice to turn to God in joyful praise.

Use the scriptures and examples given in this book to bring the presence of God into your daily life. Praise is a strong spiritual weapon that will confound your enemies and glorify God. Plus, it will be a powerful witness to those around you as you walk through trials with an attitude of praise.

Praise = The expressed glorification of God. Praise fills our lives with the presence and glory of God!

Psalms 22:3: *God inhabits the praise of his people.*

Chapter 21

Let the Praise Begin

Whosoever sacrifices praise glorifies me; and to him that orders his ways aright I will show the salvation of God.

Psalm 50:23 (Jubilee Bible)

Slave Spirituals

My ancestors endured overwhelming mental and emotional stress and anguish, and they did it with praise! They didn't talk about their circumstances, but rather sang to a God who was greater than what they saw or how they were being mistreated. They had a kingdom focus, and it was reflected in the words of their spiritual songs. For example:

"I keep so busy working for the Kingdom,
I keep so busy working for the Kingdom,
I keep so busy working for the Kingdom
I ain't got time to die.
Because it takes all of my time to praise my Jesus,
All of my time to praise my Lord,
And if I don't praise Him the rocks are going to cry out
Glory and Honor. Glory and Honor.
Ain't got time to die."

or

"I woke up this morning with my mind stayed on Jesus!"

The songs they sang took them through days and years of hard times and oppression, because they had a greater assurance of faith. Psalm 66:17:

> *I cried to him for help; I praised him with songs.* (GNT)
>
> *I cried out to Him with my mouth, and His praise was on my tongue.* (NIV)

> *"Blessed assurance, Jesus is mine.*
> *O what a foretaste of glory divine.*
> *Heir of salvation, purchased of God,*
> *Born of his spirit, washed in his blood.*
> *This is my story, this is my song,*
> *Praising my Savior all the day long.*
> *This is my story, this is my song,*
> *Praising my Savior all the day long."*

Praise Plan

For 21 days, get specific about praising God according to His Word. Praise and bless Him first with the fruit of your lips, and acknowledge His supreme love, power, mercy, wisdom, and grace before you make your petitions known or ask for anything.

Set your alarm to include praise time with reminders. At first it may be difficult for you to carve out time from your schedule. My suggestion is that you praise at the start of your regular prayer time. If no regular prayer time, then before, during, or after your meals. My personal favorites: when you go to the bathroom, when you shower, while you get dressed, as you shave or comb your hair, as you drive, while you study, and while you work. God is pleased whenever you praise him.

Read the Bible. Look up the scriptures that address your concern, and memorize them. Then repeat them out loud throughout the day. I would put several scriptures together and rap them to myself in a song. For example, in dealing with fear:

The Lord is my light and my salvation;
Whom shall, I fear?
The Lord is the strength of my life;
Of whom shall I be afraid?
In the time of trouble, He will hide me.
He will stretch out His hand against my enemies;
The Lord is my shepherd; I will fear no evil.
I will not fear evil! I will not fear! I will not fear evil!

I would sing,

I can do all things through Christ who strengthens me.
Yes, I can do all things.
All things through Christ who strengthens me.

Then, as instructed in Philippians 4:4-6, I would not allow myself to be anxious about anything. I would pray about everything, yielding my will, desiring that God would be glorified, and making my requests and petitions to Him. I postured myself to always be thankful and express my gratitude.

The 21-day practice will help you deliberately focus on praising God daily and meditating on His Word to give you good success. The blessing of *Praise Therapy* is that you customize it to **your needs**. You will find that God, by the power of His Holy Spirit, begins to sooth and minister to all the needs in your body, soul, and spirit.

My prayer is that every day you will apply *Praise Therapy* to your life. The consistent practice of personal praise will make a difference in your life. As you praise God, the power of the Holy Spirit will lead and guide you into truth according to the desires and needs of your own heart, just as He did for me. God is no respecter of persons; what He did for me He will do for you.

Appendix

"Every Praise Is to Our God." Hezekiah Walker

I've included in this appendix examples of daily praises to God. I've listed 114 scriptures from the Bible to praise God with. There are many more, and you're welcome to use any and all as you choose.

Rx: Use the scriptures in this section for daily *Praise Therapy*. The recommended minimum dosage is 3x per day, preferably morning, noon, and evening. Once you develop the practice of *Praise Therapy*, you will find that it becomes a familiar and effortless part of your daily routine. David expressed that he praised God seven times a day, Psalm 119:164:

> *Seven times a day I praise You because of Your righteous judgments.*

The meaning of judgments in this psalm = God's rules of divine administration for mankind.

Your daily dose can be adjusted, depending on your individual need. These scriptures can be taken into your heart and mind as frequently and in the amount that meets your spiritual need.

When your thoughts are filled with praise you will have the very presence of God and the mind of Christ with you. His mind is steadfast. His mind is unmovable, unanxious, undepressed, always trusting, always hoping, and always loving.

My personal testimony is that God restored my soul back to Him through praise by the giving me wisdom and understanding with the insight that He is always to be praised. With *Praise Therapy* I have transitioned through and out of great anxiety, deep depression, and dreadful fears. It is my sincere prayer that you will be blessed to have the same experience.

Praise Scriptures

Exodus 15:2	*The LORD is my strength and my defense; he has become my salvation. He is my God, and I will praise him, my father's God, and I will exalt him.*
Deuteronomy 32:3	*I will proclaim the name of the LORD. Oh, praise the greatness of our God!*
Judges 5:3	*Hear this, you kings! Listen, you rulers! I, even I, will sing to the LORD; I will praise the LORD, the God of Israel, in song.*
2 Samuel 22:4	*I call to the LORD, who is worthy of praise, and I am saved from my enemies.*
2 Samuel 22:47	*The LORD lives! Praise be to my Rock! Exalted be my God, the Rock, my Savior!*
2 Samuel 22:50	*Therefore, I will praise You, O LORD, among the nations; I will sing the praises of Your name.*
1 Kings 8:56	*Praise be to the LORD, who has given rest to his people Israel just as he promised. Not one word has failed of all the good promises he gave through his servant Moses.*
1 Chron. 16:8	*Give praise to the LORD, proclaim his name; make known among the nations what he has done.*

1 Chron. 16:9	*Sing to him, sing praise to him; tell of all his wonderful acts.*
1 Chron. 16:34	*Give thanks to the LORD, for he is good; his love endures forever.*
1 Chron. 16:35	*Cry out, "Save us, O God our Savior; gather us and deliver us from the nations, that we may give thanks to Your holy name, and glory in Your praise."*
1 Chron. 16:36	*Praise be to the LORD, the God of Israel, from everlasting to everlasting. Then all the people said "Amen" and "Praise the LORD."*
1 Chron. 23:30	*They were also to stand every morning to thank and praise the LORD. They were to do the same in the evening.*
1 Chron. 29:10	*David praised the LORD in the presence of the whole assembly, saying, "Praise be to You, LORD, the God of our father Israel, from everlasting to everlasting ..."*
1 Chron. 29:13	*Now, our God, we give You thanks, and praise Your glorious name.*
2 Chron. 5:13a	*The trumpeters and musicians joined in unison to give praise and thanks to the LORD. Accompanied by trumpets, cymbals and other instruments, the singers raised their voices in praise to the LORD and sang: "He is good; his love endures forever."*

2 Chron. 20:21	*After consulting the people, Jehoshaphat appointed men to sing to the LORD and to praise him for the splendor of his holiness as they went out at the head of the army, saying: "Give thanks to the LORD, for his love endures forever."*
Psalm 5:11	*But let all who take refuge in You be glad; let them ever sing for joy. Spread Your protection over them, that those who love Your name may rejoice in You.*
Psalm 7:17	*I will give thanks to the LORD because of his righteousness and will sing praise to the name of the LORD Most High.*
Psalm 9:1	*I will praise You Lord with all my heart, I will tell of all the marvelous things You have done.*
Psalm 9:2	*I will be filled with joy because of You. I will sing praise to Your name, O Most High.*
Psalm 9:11	*Sing praises to the LORD, enthroned in Zion; proclaim among the nations what he has done.*
Psalm 13:6	*I will sing to the LORD, for he has been good to me.*
Psalm 16:7	*I will praise the LORD, who counsels me; even at night my heart instructs me.*

Psalm 18:3	*I call to the LORD, who is worthy of praise, and I am saved from my enemies.*
Psalm 18:49	*Therefore, I will praise You among the nations, O LORD, I will sing praises to Your name.*
Psalm 22:22	*I will declare Your name to my brothers; in the congregation I will praise You.*
Psalm 28:6	*Praise be to the LORD, for he has heard my cry for mercy.*
Psalm 32:11	*Rejoice in the LORD and be glad, You righteous; sing, all You who are upright in heart!*
Psalm 33:1	*Sing joyfully to the LORD, You righteous; it is fitting for the upright to praise him.*
Psalm 34:1	*I will bless the LORD at all times; his praise will always be on my lips.*
Psalm 35:18	*I will give You thanks in the great assembly; among throngs of people I will praise You.*
Psalm 35:28	*My tongue will speak of Your righteousness and of Your praises, all day long.*
Psalm 40:3	*He put a new song in my mouth, a hymn of praise to our God. Many will see and fear and put their trust in the LORD.*

Psalm 42:11	*Why are you downcast, O my soul? Why so disturbed within me? Put your hope in God, for I will yet praise him, my Savior and my God.*
Psalm 44:8	*In God we make our boast all day long, and we will praise Your name forever. Selah.*
Psalm 47:1	*Clap your hands, all you nations; shout to God with cries of joy.*
Psalm 47:6	*Sing praises to God, sing praises; sing praises to our King, sing praises.*
Psalm 48:1	*Great is the LORD, and most worthy of praise, in the city of our God, his holy mountain.*
Psalm 51:15	*O LORD open my lips, and my mouth will declare Your praise.*
Psalm 52:9	*I will praise You forever for what You have done; in Your name I will hope, for Your name is good. I will praise You in the presence of Your saints.*
Psalm 54:6	*I will sacrifice a freewill offering to You; I will praise Your name, O LORD, for it is good.*
Psalm 56:4	*In God, whose word I praise, in God I trust; I will not be afraid. What can mortal man do to me?*
Psalm 56:10	*In God, whose word I praise, in the LORD, whose word I praise.*

Psalm 57:9	*I will praise You, O LORD, among the nations; I will sing of You among the peoples.*
Psalm 63:3	*Because Your love is better than life, my lips will glorify You.*
Psalm 63:4	*I will praise You as long as I live, and in Your name, I will lift up my hands.*
Psalm 63:5	*My soul will be satisfied as with the richest of foods; with singing lips my mouth will praise You.*
Psalm 66:2	*Sing the glory of his name; make his praise glorious!*
Psalm 66:8	*Praise our God, O peoples, let the sound of his praise be heard.*
Psalm 67:3	*May the peoples praise You, O God; may all the peoples praise You.*
Psalm 68:19	*Praise be to the LORD, to God our Savior, who daily bears our burdens. Selah.*
Psalm 69:30	*I will praise God's name in song and glorify him with thanksgiving.*
Psalm 71:8	*My mouth is filled with Your praise, declaring Your splendor all day long.*
Psalm 71:14	*But as for me, I will always have hope; I will praise You more and more.*

Psalm 74:21	*Do not let the oppressed retreat in disgrace; may the poor and needy praise Your name.*
Psalm 79:13	*Then we Your people, the sheep of Your pasture will praise You forever; from generation to generation we will recount Your praise.*
Psalm 92:1	*It is good to praise the LORD and make music to Your name, O Most High: (NKJV).*
Psalm 96:2	*Sing to the LORD, praise his name; proclaim his salvation day after day.*
Psalm 97:12	*Rejoice in the LORD, You who are righteous, and praise his holy name.*
Psalm 99:3	*Let them praise Your great and awesome name—he is holy.*
Psalm 103:1	*Praise the LORD, O my soul; all my inmost being, praise his holy name.*
Psalm 100:4-5	*Enter his gates with thanksgiving and his courts with praise; give thanks to him and praise his name. For the LORD is good and his love endures forever; his faithfulness continues through all generations.*
Psalm 103:2-3	*Praise the LORD, O my soul, and forget not all his benefits.*

Psalm 103:20-22	*Praise the LORD, you his angels, you mighty ones who do his bidding, who obey his word. Praise the LORD, all his heavenly hosts, you his servants who do his will. Praise the LORD, all his works everywhere in his dominion. Praise the LORD, O my soul.*
Psalm 104:1	*Praise the LORD, O my soul. O LORD, my God, You are very great; You are clothed with splendor and majesty.*
Psalm 104:33	*I will sing to the LORD all my life; I will sing praise to my God as long as I live.*
Psalm 105:1	*Give praise to the LORD, proclaim his name; make known among the nations what he has done.*
Psalm 105:2	*Sing to him, sing praise to him; tell of all his wonderful acts.*
Psalm 106:1	*Praise the LORD. Give thanks to the LORD, for he is good; his love endures forever.*
Psalm 106:2	*Who can proclaim the mighty acts of the LORD or fully declare his praise?*
Psalm 106:12	*Then they believed his promises and sang his praise.*
Psalm 106:48	*Praise be to the LORD, the God of Israel, from everlasting to everlasting. Let all the people say, "Amen!" Praise the LORD.*

Psalm 107:8	*Let them give thanks to the LORD for his unfailing love and his wonderful deeds for mankind.*
Psalm 113:3	*From the rising of the sun to the place where it sets, the name of the LORD is to be praised.*
Psalm 117:1	*Praise the LORD, all you nations; extol him, all you peoples.*
Psalm 117:2	*For great is his love toward us, and the faithfulness of the LORD endures forever. Praise the LORD.*
Psalm 118:28	*You are my God, and I will praise You; You are my God, and I will exalt You.*
Psalm 119:7	*I will praise You with an upright heart as I learn Your righteous laws.*
Psalm 119:12	*Praise be to You, O LORD; teach me Your decrees.*
Psalm 119:108	*Accept, O LORD, the willing praise of my mouth, and teach me Your laws.*
Psalm 119:175	*Let me live that I may praise You, and may Your laws sustain me.*
Psalm 134:1	*Praise the LORD, all you servants of the LORD who minister by night in the house of the LORD.*
Psalm 134:2	*Lift up your hands in the sanctuary and praise the LORD.*

Psalm 135:1	*Praise the LORD. Praise the name of the LORD; praise him, you servants of the LORD.*
Psalm 135:3	*Praise the LORD, for the LORD is good; sing praise to his name, for that is pleasant.*
Psalm 138:1	*I will praise You, O LORD, with all my heart; before the "gods" I will sing Your praise.*
Psalm 139:14	*I praise You because I am fearfully and wonderfully made; Your works are wonderful; I know that full well.*
Psalm 145:1	*I will exalt You, my God the King; I will praise Your name for ever and ever.*
Psalm 145:2	*Every day I will praise You and extol Your name for ever and ever.*
Psalm 145:21	*My mouth will speak in praise of the LORD. Let every creature praise his holy name for ever and ever.*
Psalm 147:1	*Praise the LORD. How good it is to sing praises to our God, how pleasant and fitting to praise him!*
Psalm 150:1	*Praise the LORD. Praise God in his sanctuary; praise him in his mighty heavens.*
Psalm 150:2	*Praise him for his acts of power; praise him for his surpassing greatness.*

Psalm 150:6	*Let everything that has breath praise the LORD. Praise the LORD.*
Isaiah 25:1	*O LORD, You are my God; I will exalt You and praise Your name, for in perfect faithfulness You have done marvelous things, things planned long ago.*
Luke 18:43	*Immediately he received his sight and followed Jesus, praising God. When all the people saw it, they also praised God.*
Luke 19:37	*When he came near the place where the road goes down the Mount of Olives, the whole crowd of disciples began joyfully to praise God in loud voices for all the miracles they had seen:*
Luke 24:53	*And they stayed continually at the temple, praising God.*
Romans 15:7	*Accept one another, then, just as Christ accepted you, in order to bring praise to God.*
Romans 15:11	*And again, "Praise the LORD, all you Gentiles, and sing praises to him, all you peoples."*
Ephesians 1:3	*Praise be to the God and Father of our LORD Jesus Christ, who has blessed us in the heavenly realms with every spiritual blessing in Christ.*

Ephesians 5:19-20	*Speak to one another with psalms, hymns and spiritual songs. Sing and make music in your heart to the LORD.*
1 Timothy 1:17	*Now to the King eternal, immortal, invisible, the only God, be honor and glory for ever and ever. Amen.*
Hebrews 13:15	*Through Jesus, therefore, let us continually offer to God a sacrifice of praise—the fruit of lips that confess his name.*
James 5:13	*Is anyone among you in trouble? Let them pray. Is anyone happy? Let them sing songs of praise.*
1 Peter 1:3	*Praise be to the God and Father of our LORD Jesus Christ! In his great mercy he has given us new birth into a living hope through the resurrection of Jesus Christ from the dead.*
1 Peter 2:9	*But you are a chosen people, a royal priesthood, a holy nation, a people belonging to God, that you may declare the praises of him who called you out of darkness into his wonderful light.*
1 Peter 4:16	*However, if you suffer as a Christian, do not be ashamed, but praise God that you bear that name.*

Revelation 5:12	*In a loud voice they sang: Worthy is the Lamb, who was slain, to receive power and wealth and wisdom and strength and honor and glory and praise!*
Revelation 5:13	*Then I heard every creature in heaven and on earth and under the earth and on the sea, and all that is in them, singing: "To him who sits on the throne and to the Lamb be praise and honor and glory and power, forever and ever!"*
Revelation 7:12	*Amen! Praise and glory and wisdom and thanks and honor and power and strength be to our God for ever and ever. Amen.*
Revelation 19:1	*After this I heard what sounded like the roar of a great multitude in heaven shouting: "Hallelujah! Salvation and glory and power belong to our God, ..."*
Revelation 19:5	*Then a voice came from the throne, saying: "Praise our God, all you his servants, you who fear him, both small and great!"*

All Scriptures in this Appendix are from the New International Version of the Bible unless otherwise noted.

Author's Biographical Sketch

Jeraleen Peterson, LCSW, writes under her maiden name, Jeraleen M. Ray, in tribute to her parents, who both made great sacrifices for her to live and survive. *Praise Therapy* is her first book and is "joyfully" dedicated to those who are struggling to find hope and answers that will produce a healthy, "sane" mentality for them.

In *Praise Therapy*, she shares how she used biblical wisdom and integrated biblical mindfulness, in what she calls "praise therapy," to address the down pull of shame, anxiety, depression, and fear while facing the challenges of single parenting, multiple deaths, poverty, and the trauma of sexual and emotional abuse.

Jeraleen is an author, speaker, biblical teacher, and human encourager with over 40 years of experience as a counselor, therapist, and mentor. She is a licensed clinical social worker, the mother of four children, and grandmother of six. Her mission and purpose are to help develop the skills of resilience and perseverance in as many human's lives as possible for the praise and glory of God.

Author 's Contact Information

Jeraleen Peterson is available for speaking at your event. You can contact her using any of the following:

Email: *prazetherapy@gmail.com*

Instagram: *@praze.therapy*

Twitter: *Wisdom Tree Counseling*
@JherisWisdom

Facebook: https://www.facebook.com/praze.therapy

Made in the USA
Lexington, KY
28 September 2019